DATE DUE

Demco, Inc. 38-293

GREAT MINDS OF SCIENCE

Isaac Newton
The Greatest Scientist of All Time

Margaret J. Anderson

Enslow Publishers, Inc.

44 Fadem Road   PO Box 38
Box 699   Aldershot
Springfield, NJ 07081   Hants GU12 6BP
USA   UK

Library of Congress Cataloging-in-Publication Data

Anderson, Margaret Jean, 1931–
    Isaac Newton : the greatest scientist of all time / [by
Margaret J. Anderson].
       p. cm. — (Great minds of science)
    Includes bibliographical references and index.
    Summary: A biography of the seventeenth-century English
scientist who formulated the theory of gravity.
    ISBN 0-89490-681-X
    1. Newton, Isaac, Sir, 1642–1727—Juvenile literature. 2. Physicists—
Great Britain—Biography—Juvenile literature. [1. Newton, Isaac, Sir,
1642–1727. 2. Scientists.] I. Title. II. Series.
QC16.N7A53 1996
530'.092—dc20
[B]   96-4958
                                              CIP
                                              AC

Printed in the United States of America.

10 9 8 7 6 5 4 3 2

Illustration Credits: Margaret J. Anderson, pp. 6, 16, 20, 23, 24, 28,
33, 43, 45, 53, 66, 70, 74, 83, 94, 99, 104, 107; Stephen Delisle, pp.
18, 47, 50, 55, 59, 85, 114, 116; Library of Congress, pp. 8, 11, 31,
76, 77, 87, 92; National Trust, p. 61; Trinity College Library, Cambridge University, p. 38.

Cover Photo Credits: Science VU/Visuals Unlimited (Background);
Library of Congress (Inset).

Contents

"On the Shoulders of Giants"

ON CHRISTMAS DAY, 1642, HANNAH NEWTON gave birth to a baby boy. She named him Isaac after his father, but there was no father on hand to welcome the new baby. Isaac Newton, Senior, had died in October.

Hannah's baby was born early. He was so small that she could have fitted him inside a quart jug. He was so weak that she had to fix a little pillow around his neck to hold up his head. On the day he was born, two women who were helping Hannah went over to a neighbor's house to fetch some medicine. They saw no need to hurry. They

Isaac Newton was born on Christmas Day 1642 in Woolsthorpe Manor.

were so sure that little Isaac would not live until they got back that they rested on a wall.[1]

This baby, who got off to such a shaky start, grew up to have one of the best minds of all time. Isaac Newton was a genius. He invented a branch of mathematics called calculus. He designed the reflecting telescope. He figured out the principle of gravity. He proved that white light contains the colors of the rainbow.

If Isaac Newton had come up with any one of these great ideas, he would have been famous. It is truly amazing that one person could do so many things. When he was an old man, someone asked him how he had done it. He answered, "If I have seen further than most men, it is by standing on the shoulders of giants."[2]

Newton's "giants" included great men like Copernicus, Kepler, Galileo, and Descartes.

Copernicus was a Polish monk who studied mathematics, medicine, and astronomy. Shortly before he died in 1543, Copernicus published a book on the movement of the planets. He said that the planets and the earth circle the sun. This

Isaac Newton had one of the greatest minds of all time.

went against the teachings of Aristotle, a Greek scholar who lived in the fourth century B.C. Aristotle pictured the universe as a series of hollow spheres arranged around the earth. He shaped people's thinking for the next fifteen hundred years. It took courage for Copernicus to challenge an idea that had been around for so long. People did not like what he told them. They wanted to go on believing that the earth was the center of the universe.

Galileo was another scientist who questioned some of Aristotle's teachings. He was born in Pisa, Italy, in 1564. Today, science and experiments go together. This was not always the case. Galileo was one of the first scientists to try to prove a theory by doing experiments. Aristotle thought that if two different weights were dropped from the same height, the heavier would hit the ground first. Galileo tested this by dropping several weights from the Leaning Tower of Pisa. They fell at the same speed. He noticed that the longer an object falls, the faster it falls. Those facts later helped Newton develop his law of gravity.

One of Galileo's ideas came to him during a church service. A big lamp hanging from the cathedral ceiling was swaying in a draft. Using his pulse, Galileo timed the swings. He discovered that when the swings got shorter, they took the same amount of time. Galileo then went on to invent the pendulum clock. This advanced the study of physics and astronomy. Solving problems in these subjects often requires an accurate way of measuring time.

Even though some of Galileo's ideas came to him in church, the Church did not like his ideas. In 1632, Galileo published a book in which he agreed with Copernicus that the earth travels around the sun. After his book came out, Galileo was brought to Rome before a church court called the Inquisition. He was forced to deny his work. He spent the rest of his life in the countryside away from places of learning. Galileo died in January 1642. Isaac Newton was born in December of that year.

Johannes Kepler, a German astronomer, agreed that the planets orbit the sun. He did not

Johannes Kepler (1571–1630), a German astronomer, studied the motion of the planets.

think, as Copernicus did, that they move in perfect circles. He said that each planet travels in a flattened oval orbit called an ellipse. He also said that the speed of a planet varies with its distance from the sun. Those ideas provided an important base for the theory of gravity.

René Descartes, another of Newton's giants, was born in France in 1596 and moved to the

Netherlands in 1628 where people were open to new ideas. Descartes was interested in philosophy and mathematics. He was a great doubter. He claimed that the only thing he could be sure about was his own existence. He said it in Latin: "*Cogito ergo sum*" ("I think, therefore I am"). Educated people all knew Latin in those days.

Descartes came up with the mathematical idea of coordinates, which are used in charts and graphs. Graphs can show how different quantities are related. For example, by plotting the weights and heights of children, you can see that children tend to get heavier as they grow taller. Their weights and heights are related. Descartes's writings opened Newton's eyes to the wonders of mathematics.

Newton learned about the work of the great scientists of Europe by studying their books. He knew many of the great English scientists in person. He met them in London at the Royal Society, where scientists shared new ideas. Edmund Halley, who has a comet named after him, was a member. So was Christopher Wren, who built St. Paul's Cathedral in London. Robert

Boyle and Robert Hooke were also members. Boyle is sometimes called the father of chemistry. Hooke, like Newton, had a brilliant mind for physics.

Although Isaac Newton knew those great men, he did not always get along with them.

"A Sober, Silent, Thinking Lad"

ISAAC NEWTON'S GENIUS CANNOT BE explained by his family background; nor can it be explained by his upbringing. Isaac's father, like his father and grandfather before him, was a simple farmer. In his will, he left Woolsthorpe Manor in Lincolnshire to his wife. The will was signed with an X. He did not know how to write his own name.

Hannah Newton's side of the family had more education. She could write. Her two brothers had been to college and were clergymen. They lived nearby and gave the young widow advice and friendship.

Although Hannah Newton had her own home and an income from the farm, bringing up her child alone was not easy. Those were difficult times in England. Civil war had broken out in August 1642. Families were divided, and soldiers roamed the countryside. Battles were fought not far from Woolsthorpe Manor.

The civil war had started because King Charles I could not get along with Parliament. He decided to rule without it. Oliver Cromwell, a Puritan, led a rebellion against the king. The war lasted six and a half years, ending in January 1649. King Charles I was tried for treason and was beheaded two weeks later. Cromwell became Lord Protector.

Early in 1646, while the civil war was still raging, Hannah Newton married Barnabas Smith. Her new husband was a clergyman. He lived in a village about a mile and a half from Woolsthorpe Manor. He was much older than Hannah Newton, but he was wealthy and well educated. It was a good match for Hannah Newton, but things did not go well for little Isaac.

Charles I was executed in 1649 at the end of the English Civil War. Oliver Cromwell became the Lord Protector, and ruled Britain for the next nine years.

When his mother married Smith, Isaac was left behind at Woolsthorpe Manor. He was only three years old. His grandmother moved in to take care of him.

Isaac seems to have been a lonely little boy. Woolsthorpe Manor was a modest farmhouse in the country. A number of relatives lived in the area, but we do not know whether or not they came to visit. Isaac had his own bedroom in the attic. Sometimes he amused himself by drawing on the walls. He carved on the wooden windowsill. When he was around five, he went to the village school, where he learned to read and write.

When Isaac was ten his stepfather died and his mother came back to live at Woolsthorpe. She did not come alone; she now had three more children. Mary was four and a half, Benjamin was two, and little Hannah was one.

Two years later, Isaac was sent off to grammar school in Grantham. Grantham was a market town, seven miles from Woolsthorpe. That was too far for Isaac to travel each day, so he stayed with the Clark family. They lived on the High

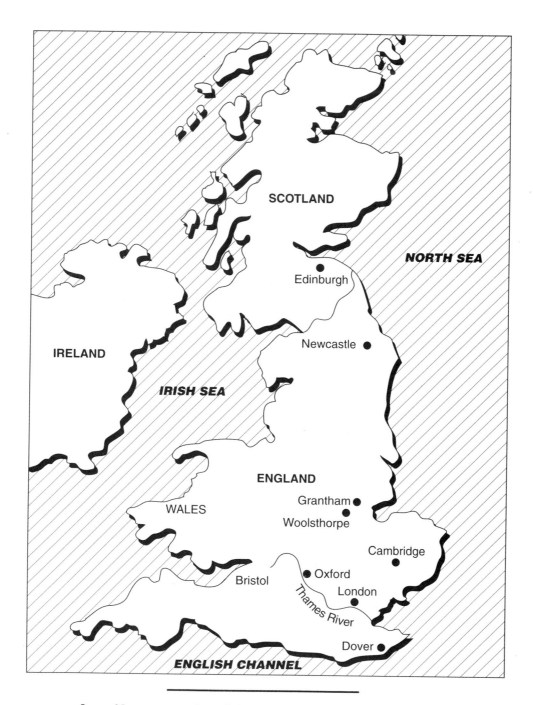

SCOTLAND

NORTH SEA

Edinburgh

IRELAND

Newcastle

IRISH SEA

ENGLAND

Grantham

WALES

Woolsthorpe

Cambridge

Bristol

Oxford

London

Thames River

Dover

ENGLISH CHANNEL

Isaac Newton spent his whole life in England. By the time of his death, he was known throughout Europe as a great scientist.

Street next to the George Inn. Mr. Clark ran an apothecary shop (drugstore). Isaac was interested in the medicines Mr. Clark prepared. In this way, he learned some chemistry, which was helpful to him later on. He also gathered herbs and learned their uses.

Mrs. Clark had two sons and a daughter from an earlier marriage. Isaac didn't get along with the boys, Edward and Arthur Storer. He preferred the daughter's company. Some of what we know about Newton's boyhood is from her memories. When she was eighty-two, she was interviewed by William Stukeley, who was writing Isaac Newton's biography. She said that Isaac was always a "sober, silent, thinking lad." She remembered him making "little tables and other utensils for her, and her play fellows, to set their babys and trinkets on."[1]

Isaac is said to have "entertain'd a passion for her when they grew up."[2] Miss Storer is the only hint of a romance in Isaac's long life, and we do not even know her first name. He stayed friendly with her over the years. After she was married,

Grantham Grammar School

Isaac visited her and her husband whenever he was in Grantham.

Isaac did not get along any better with the boys at school than he did with the Storer brothers at home. He was still small for his age, and he was used to being alone. His schoolmates found him "too cunning."[3] He seldom joined them in their games, but when he did, he made sure he won. One windy day, the boys held a jumping contest. By timing his jump to match an extra-strong gust, Isaac jumped the farthest. He was already putting physics to work!

He also used his cunning in making kites. He worked out the best place to fasten the string, and how long the tail should be. One time he tied a paper lantern with a candle in it to the tail of a kite. He flew it in the dark and "wonderfully affrighted" the neighbors.[4] They talked about the strange light over their mugs of ale.

The schoolmaster, Mr. Stokes, was a good teacher. Even so, Isaac did not do well in his new school. He sat at the bottom of the lowest class. Perhaps the village school had not prepared him for grammar school. More likely, he did not find the lessons interesting. Latin was an important subject because students needed to know it to read textbooks and scientific papers. They were all written in Latin. No matter what language was spoken at home—French, German, English, Spanish, or Italian—scholars were able to read the works of the learned people in the rest of Europe. Isaac Newton later wrote his most famous book, the *Principia,* in Latin.

The Bible and Bible history were other important school subjects. Mathematics, on the other hand, was not important; students learned only basic arithmetic. Nor did they study current affairs, although those were restless times. As Lord Protector of England, Oliver Cromwell was not getting along any better with Parliament than Charles I had.

Isaac's attitude in class took a turn for the better after a fight with Arthur Storer. Arthur seems to have been the school bully. One morning, Arthur kicked Isaac in the stomach. After school, Isaac challenged Arthur to a fight.

Isaac Newton carved his name on his desk.

The two boys headed for the churchyard. Young Stokes, the schoolmaster's son, went along to cheer the boys on. Isaac was smaller than Arthur, but he had more spirit. Soon Arthur had had enough. Stokes told Isaac that he should rub the bully's nose against the church wall. So Isaac "pulled him along by the ears and thrust his face against the side of the church."[5]

Isaac was the clear winner. However, that did

Plaster cast of a sundial which Newton carved when he was 9 years old. This is now in Colsterworth church.

This is a replica of the sundial that Isaac Newton carved on a wall when he was nine years old.

not satisfy him. He decided to beat his enemy in schoolwork as well. He began to study hard. He soon rose to the top of the class. Beating the school bully, though, did not suddenly make Isaac popular. He still spent most of his time alone.

Isaac was fond of drawing. He continued to draw on walls. His attic room was decorated with sketches of birds, beasts, men, ships, and plants. He drew shapes, such as circles and triangles. No one seems to have minded. The drawings were not scrubbed off.

Like other boys, Isaac carved his name on his school desk. One of his carvings shows the beginning of his genius. When he was just nine years old, he carved a sundial on a wall at Woolsthorpe Manor. While he was with the Clarks, he made sundials all over the house. He marked the hours, the half hours, and the quarter hours with pegs. He tied strings between the pegs to measure the shadows on different days. He could tell the shortest and the longest days and the time of the equinoxes.

Isaac was aware of the movement of shadows all his life. When he walked into a sunny room, he could tell the time from the position of shadows without looking at a clock. This, however, did not keep him from making clocks. While he lived with the Clarks, he made a water clock. It worked by dripping water through a small hole. It kept good time unless the hole was "furr'd up [blocked] by impuritys in the water."[6]

While Isaac was in Grantham, a new wind-powered mill was built on the edge of town. Windmills were not common in that part of the country, so many of the townspeople showed up to watch its progress. Isaac was among them. He watched so carefully that he was able to make an exact model of it when he got home. He used cloth for sails. He set up his model on the roof. Then he came up with an improvement. Instead of wind power, he used a treadmill run by a mouse to turn the sails. People dropped in to see Isaac's "mouse miller."[7] A neighboring farmer gave Isaac corn for his mouse.

When Isaac was sixteen, his mother said it was time for him to come home. She needed him to run the farm. Isaac, however had no interest in farming. His mind was still on models and inventions. Instead of watching the sheep, he built waterwheels in the brook. They were good waterwheels, with dams and sluices. Meantime, the sheep were eating the neighbor's grain.

On market days, Isaac bribed the servant to drop him off at the first corner past the manor. While the servant sold the produce and bought supplies, Isaac made models or read a book. If he did go into town, rather than keep his mind on what he should be doing, he went back to the Clarks' and spent the day reading in his old room.

Outside Grantham, the road was very steep. It was the custom to lead horses up the hill, rather than to ride. One day, when Isaac reached the top, he forgot to get back on his horse. Lost in thought, he trudged on for five miles, leading his horse. Another time, when the horse slipped out of the bridle and went home by itself, Isaac did not notice. He continued to walk with the bridle in his hand.

The servants all thought that young Isaac was foolish, and his mother did not know what to do with him. Luckily, his old schoolmaster, Mr. Stokes, was now living in a nearby village. He told Hannah Smith that Isaac's brain was wasted on a

Although Isaac Newton preferred reading to going to the market, a shopping center in Grantham bears his name.

farm. He said Isaac should go back to grammar school to fit himself for Cambridge University. Mr. Stokes even offered to pay his fees and said that Isaac could stay with him.

It was a good solution all around. Isaac was back among his beloved books. His mother could relax, and the servants "rejoic'd at parting with him, declaring, he was fit for nothing but the 'Versity."[8]

A Student at Cambridge

OLIVER CROMWELL DIED IN 1658. HE HAD been a stern but honest ruler. His son Richard took over, but he did not possess his father's strong character. He resigned after one year. England decided to have a king again. Charles II was crowned in 1660.

This period, known as the Restoration, is an important time in English history. It is also an important time in the history of science. Charles II was interested in advances in science. In 1662, he gave his backing to the founding of the Royal Society. Before there were scientific journals, it was hard for people to keep up with new ideas.

Charles II (1630–1685) was a strong supporter of science and the Royal Society.

Meetings of the Royal Society provided a setting where scientists could share their discoveries. The first members included the architect Christopher Wren and the writer Samuel Pepys. Robert Hooke was chosen to be in charge of doing experiments.

The year before the Royal Society was formed, another event happened that also is important in the history of science. Isaac Newton enrolled at Cambridge University. Young Isaac must have been both excited and nervous when he first saw the spires of Cambridge on the skyline. Compared with Grantham, Cambridge was a big city. The university buildings were impressive. They were old even then. There is no record of what Isaac thought, but we know from his account book that it took him three days to get there. We also know that when he arrived, he bought supplies. He bought a lock for his desk, a notebook, ink, a pound of candles, and a chamber pot. Ink and candles appear often in Isaac's account book. He sometimes stayed up all night reading, studying, and taking notes.

Cambridge University is divided into colleges.

Trinity College of Cambridge University was founded in 1546 by Henry VIII.

Isaac enrolled in Trinity College. He started out as a sizar. Sizars paid lower fees, and they acted as servants to the wealthier students and teachers. Isaac, however, was not a servant.

It is surprising that Isaac chose to be a sizar.

His mother, Hannah Smith, had a good income and could have afforded to pay Isaac's fees. She owned Woolsthorpe Manor, and she had inherited money and land from her second husband, Barnabas Smith. Maybe she thought he would get more out of his education if he worked for it. Maybe she was annoyed that he had not chosen to be a farmer.

Being a sizar set Isaac apart from the other students. He made no close friends, but then he had made no close friends at grammar school, either. Back in the seventeenth century, students faced some of the same problems they do today. Isaac had roommate troubles. He was studious, but his roommate liked to have parties. One evening, to get away from the noise, Isaac went for a walk. While he was out, he met John Wickins, and they began talking. They found that both were wandering around in the dark for the same reason. The answer to their problem was plain; they agreed to "shake off their present disorderly Companions and Chum together."[1] Isaac Newton and John Wickins shared rooms for many years at Cambridge. They suited one another, yet they never became close friends.

In those days, there was not a wide choice of subjects to study. College prepared young men for a career in the church or in medicine. A third choice was to become a scholar and stay on at Cambridge. Each student had a tutor who directed his studies. Isaac's tutor was Benjamin Pulleyn.

Each August, Sturbridge Fair—the biggest fair in England—came to Cambridge. A visit to this fair kindled Isaac's interest in mathematics. He bought a book on astrology at one of the stalls. To help him understand the mathematics in his new book, he then bought a geometry text by Euclid, a Greek mathematician who had lived around 300 B.C. When Isaac first read Euclid, he didn't think much of it. Instead, he turned to a very difficult modern math book by Descartes. He got bogged down after two or three pages, so he went back to the beginning. This time he got three or four pages farther before he was stuck. Back he went to the beginning. He continued in this way until he had mastered the whole book.

The mathematics professor at Cambridge was a young man in his early thirties named Isaac Barrow, who already had had a colorful career. He chose to leave the university while Cromwell was in power, and traveled through France, Italy, and Turkey, where he had many adventures. Once, when he was on a ship that was attacked by pirates, he fought them off bravely. After Charles II became king, Barrow returned to Cambridge and became a professor of mathematics. He did not realize right away that young Isaac Newton was a remarkable student.

During an exam, Professor Barrow tested Isaac on what he knew about Euclid's geometry. Isaac could not answer his questions. He was too shy to say he had been busy reading Descartes's book on the new geometry. Even if he had, Barrow might not have believed him. Understanding Descartes without first reading Euclid would seem to be impossible, but Isaac Newton could do the impossible in mathematics. While he was still a student, he developed the binomial theorem (rule). A binomial is two numbers connected by a plus or minus sign. Newton's rule provided a shortcut for multiplying a binomial by itself many times over. By the time he was twenty-two, Isaac was already going beyond other people's thinking.

Isaac took notes on everything he read. These notes form part of a collection of Newton's papers, now at Cambridge University. From these papers we know what interested him during his student days. At one point, he changed his style of handwriting so that he could take notes faster. He figured out new ways of making ink. He wrote with a feather pen. Soon after going to Cambridge, Isaac made a list of his sins, one of which was making a new pen on a Sunday.

Isaac had a book where he wrote down things that he wanted to know more about. He listed forty-five headings. Some were about general subjects, such as matter, time, and motion. Headings like "Soul" and "Sleep" show how wide his interests were. Under "Of Water and Salt" he wrote about the tides. He came up with the theory that tides were connected with the phases of the

Isaac Newton sat for this portrait around the time when he got his bachelor of arts degree.

moon. He explained their movement without ever seeing the ocean.

Isaac was fascinated by the night sky. One of the headings in his notebook was "Of the Sunn, Starrs & Planetts & Comets." He stayed up so many nights in 1664 watching a comet that he became "disordered."[2] He often forgot to eat. His cat was well fed on the food he left untouched on his plate. He kept this habit of thinking about something so hard that he forgot to eat or sleep all his life.

Some of Isaac's experiments were dangerous to himself. He once stared with his right eye at the image of the sun in a mirror. When he closed his eye, he saw colored circles. He was interested in how the circles changed color as they faded, so he tried the experiment again, and he nearly ruined his eyesight. He was soon seeing spots of color everywhere, and he had to stay in a dark room for several days to recover his sight. This cured him of looking at the sun, but it did not cure him of experimenting with his own eyes. He did so again while trying to understand the nature of light.

In the spring of 1665, Isaac earned his bachelor of arts degree. He was one of twenty-six men earning degrees. We do not know how Isaac compared with these other students, because the page in the book that shows the rankings of the students is missing. In his biography of Newton, William Stukeley claims that Isaac did not pass the first time. He had been too busy "in the solid track of learning" to study for the test.[3]

Isaac's next goal was his master of arts degree. However, in the summer of 1665, an event outside Cambridge sent Isaac back home to Woolsthorpe. Outside events could not keep him from being a scholar, though. Isaac's genius was about to burst into full bloom.

A Fruitful Vacation

TOWARD THE END OF 1664, SOME PEOPLE in London became sick. The illness started out like flu with a headache, high fever, and dizziness. This was followed by swellings in the armpits and on the neck. Within a few days, patients either died or recovered. Most died. The dreaded plague had surfaced again. There was good reason for fear. In the fourteenth century, an outbreak called the Black Death killed one in four people in Europe.

Plague is a disease of rats that is passed to people by fleas. Both rats and fleas thrived in the dirty, crowded conditions found in seventeenth-century London. The disease spread quickly. By the summer of 1665, it had claimed thirty-one thousand lives.

Samuel Pepys described the scenes of horror in his diary. Red crosses were painted on the doors of the houses of the sick. Carts were pushed through the street to the mournful cry of "Bring out your dead!" Charles II and his court left for the country. So did everyone else with somewhere to go. People fleeing London carried the sickness to other cities.

In August 1665, Cambridge University closed its doors. Many of the teachers and students had already left. Isaac Newton was at Woolsthorpe Manor. He was now twenty-two years old, and he had his bachelor of arts degree. Back home, he studied harder than ever. His next eighteen months would later be known as "the miracle years." Newton did his greatest thinking during this time. Fifty years later, he said, "In those days I was in the prime of my age for invention and minded

The great plague caused many people to flee from London. The dead were laid out on the street. Wagons travelled the city picking up the victims. They were buried in mass graves.

mathematics and philosophy more than any time since."[1]

The servants did not know that Newton was "minding mathematics" while he sat in the garden under the apple tree. They probably thought he was as idle as ever, but his mind was busy. He was thinking about gravity. The story goes that while he was sitting in the garden, an apple fell from the tree. Why did the apple fall *down,* he wondered. Why not *up,* or *sideways*? He figured that some force must be pulling the apple toward the earth. Isaac Newton had discovered the principle of gravity.

Newton did not really figure out gravity in the time it takes an apple to fall from a tree, though he himself gave us the apple legend. When he was an old man, he told the story to William Stukeley. They were drinking tea together under an apple tree in his garden. He said that he was sitting under a similar tree when the theory of gravity came to his mind. "It was occasion'd by the fall of an apple. . . "[2]

For some time before the apple fell, Newton's

This apple tree on the grounds of Woolsthorpe Manor is a direct descendant of Newton's famous tree.

thinking had been preparing him for the question of gravity. He was interested in the mathematics of motion. If something moves in a straight line at a constant speed, it is easy to figure out where it will be at any given time. For example, a car traveling along a straight road at fifty miles per hour will be fifty miles away at the end of an hour. But how do you figure out where the car will be if it speeds up or slows down? Where will it be if it is traveling around curves?

Using algebra, Newton could solve an equation to find the value of *x,* an unknown number. Finding the value of an unknown number that kept changing was a tougher problem. Newton set about looking for an answer. In doing so, he came up with a new branch of mathematics. He called it fluxions, from the word *flux,* which means "constant changing or flowing." We now call it calculus.

Late in the fall of 1665, Newton used fluxions to find the area under an open curve known as a hyperbola. The answer thrilled him so much that he took it to fifty-two places beyond the decimal.

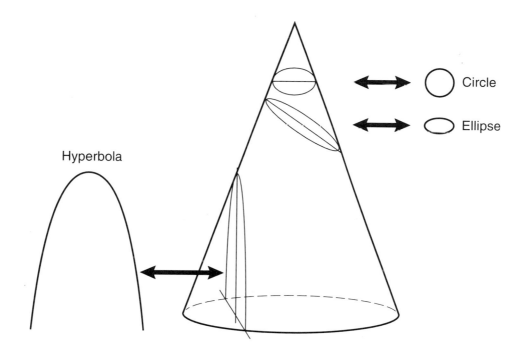

Circle

Ellipse

Hyperbola

Different shapes result from cutting a cone at different angles.

However, he did not rush out and tell everyone about this useful new branch of mathematics. Isaac Newton was always slow to share his discoveries with the world. He had to be sure he had everything right. Besides, he was impatient to explore the other new ideas that were crowding into his mind.

If Newton had told people about fluxions right away, he could have avoided a long quarrel. Ten years later, in Germany, Wilhelm Leibniz came up with more or less the same method. A great many people were drawn into the argument about who should get the credit for discovering calculus. Newton's solitary nature sometimes set him at war with himself as well as with other people. On one hand, he wanted to be left alone to do his thinking in peace. On the other hand, he wanted and needed recognition, but he always had a hard time dealing with the questions or criticism that can come with fame.

Fluxions helped Newton tackle new problems. Like many scientists before him, he was interested in the movement of the planets. Kepler's work provided a starting point for his studies.

Kepler's three laws of motion state that:

1. Each planet travels in an ellipse around the sun. The sun is at one of the focal points of the ellipse.

2. The speed of a planet traveling around the sun changes all the time. It changes in such a way that a line drawn from the center of the sun to the center of a planet sweeps over equal areas in equal lengths of time.

3. The time it takes a planet to orbit the sun is related to its distance from the sun.

Kepler's laws describe the motion of the planets. They do not explain what causes the planets to move.

Isaac Newton turned his thoughts to the moon. A moving body keeps on moving in a straight line and at the same speed unless an outside force changes its direction and speed. So why did the moon not shoot off into space? Some outside force must keep it in orbit. The apple falling from a tree provided a key to what that outside force might be. The earth was pulling the moon toward itself. At the same time as the moon was shooting off into space, it was continually falling toward the center of the earth.

Newton set out to back up his theory with mathematics. To complete his calculations, he needed to know the radius of the earth. The measurement he used was not exact. The answer did not work out as neatly as he had hoped.

Even though the calculation did not work out exactly, Newton was sure he was on the right

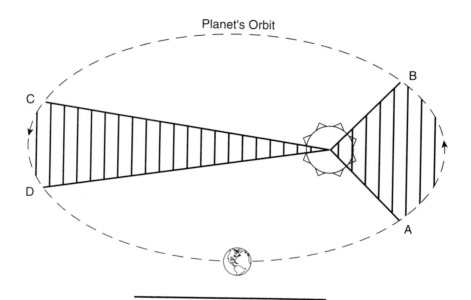

Planet's Orbit

Johannes Kepler discovered from observation that planets orbit the sun in an ellipse, not a perfect circle. Using calculus, Newton was able to prove this fact.

track. He had satisfied his own need to understand. Almost fifteen years later, he redid the calculation with the correct distance for the earth's radius. Five years after that, he shared his brilliant work with the world.

Meantime, Isaac Newton was busy solving other scientific mysteries.

Seeing the Light

ISAAC NEWTON'S DISCOVERIES ABOUT light and color started with another purchase at Sturbridge Fair; he bought a prism. He already knew that when light passes through a prism it breaks up into the colors of the rainbow. He had also seen fringes of color around objects when he looked through a telescope. The fringe of color made it harder to see an object clearly. He knew that it had something to do with the curved lens in the telescope.

Newton's first experiment with his prism was simple. He had shutters on his window. By closing

This display in Grantham Museum shows Newton experimenting with light.

them, he could darken his room. He pierced a hole in one shutter so that a beam of sunlight hit the opposite wall. Here is how he described what he did: "Having darkened my chamber, and made a small hole in my window shuts, to let in a convenient quantity of the sun's light, I placed my prism . . . [so that the light] might . . . be refracted to the opposite wall."[1]

When the prism was placed in the path of the light beam, the colors of the rainbow showed up on the wall. They were always in the same order—red, orange, yellow, green, blue, indigo, and violet. Was white light really a mixture of colors? Isaac noticed that the colors formed an oblong shape although the hole in the shutter was round. He was now looking at a math problem. What made the round beam turn into an oblong shape? The answer must be that the prism refracted (bent) the colors at different angles. It bent the blue light the most and the red light the least.

Newton did another experiment using two prisms. He placed the second prism upside down in front of the first one. The colors came together again to make white light on the back wall. By bringing the colors back together, he had produced white light. The white light was in the shape of a circle.

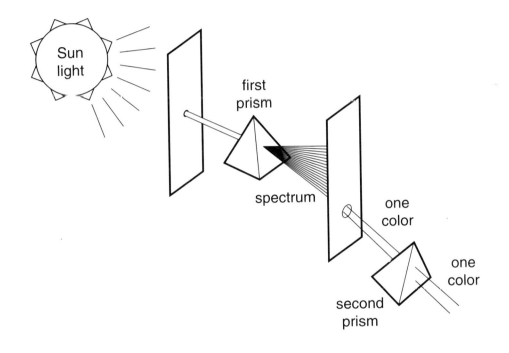

Sun light

first prism

spectrum

one color

one color

second prism

Using a single prism and a pinhole punched in a piece of wood, Newton was able to isolate one color of the spectrum. Sending the same ray of light through a second prism showed that it could not be broken down any further.

He tried another experiment. This time, he took a card with a hole in it and placed it between the two prisms, letting only red light pass through the hole. The red light then passed through the second prism. Only red showed on the back wall. He repeated this with the other colors. He was able to isolate each color in turn.

Meantime, London was facing yet another disaster. On the night of September 1, 1666, Samuel Pepys was wakened by his maid, Jane. She told him that the city was on fire. Pepys looked out of the window and then went back to bed. Fires were common in London.

The Lord Mayor was at the scene of the fire. He did not think it was anything to worry about, either. He was against pulling down houses to make a fire break. This turned out to be a costly mistake. By the next morning, three hundred houses had burned. The wind had risen, and fire was spreading in every direction through the crowded, dirty wooden buildings. The Lord Mayor now wanted houses pulled down everywhere. The fire was so fierce no one could get close to it.

The Great Fire of London burned for four nights and four days. It destroyed eighty-seven churches and over thirteen thousand homes. In time, the city would be rebuilt, but the London of Shakespeare and Queen Elizabeth I was gone. The fire also took care of the problems of rats and filth. The plague was finally over.

Cambridge University opened again in March of the following year. Isaac Newton was studying for his master of arts degree, but it was the fellowship exam in October that would really decide his future. As a fellow, he could continue to live in the university, and he could spend the rest of his life as a scholar. Fellows gave lectures and advised students, but there was also plenty of time for reading and studying.

Becoming a fellow was not based just on the results of an exam; politics were involved. Some students had letters of recommendation from the king. It also helped to have friends among the senior fellows who did the choosing. That year, there were nine places to be filled. This was more than usual because no fellowships had been given during the plague years.

When the bell tolled on October 2 to summon the new fellows, Newton was one of the nine. He must have been relieved. Without a fellowship, he would have had to return to the farm at Woolsthorpe.

Two years after Newton became a fellow, Professor Barrow resigned. He named Isaac Newton to take his place. At the age of twenty-seven, Newton was appointed as professor of mathematics. However, few people outside Cambridge knew the brilliant young professor. He still kept most of his ideas to himself.

Isaac Newton continued to be interested in light and color. He wanted to make a telescope that would not have fringes of color around the objects he was looking at. We now know that this can be done by combining lenses of different kinds of glass. Newton chose another way; he used reflecting mirrors instead of lenses. The idea of using reflecting mirrors was first suggested by James Gregory, a Scottish scientist. However, his

Gregory's Idea

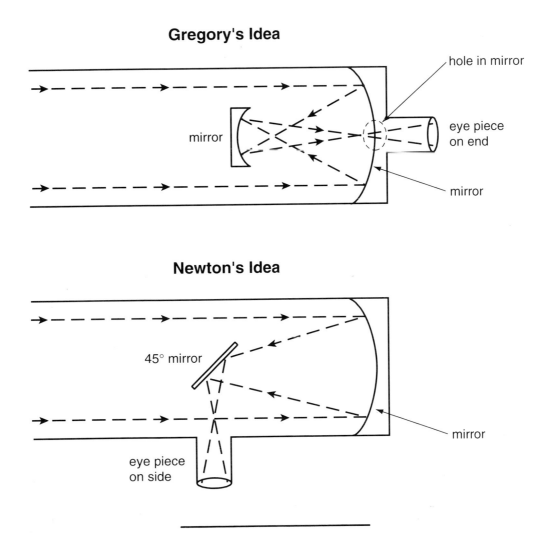

hole in mirror

mirror

eye piece
on end

mirror

Newton's Idea

45° mirror

mirror

eye piece
on side

Newton improved on Gregory's idea of using two mirrors in a telescope. By placing one mirror at an angle, Newton was able to reflect the light through a side eyepiece.

plan was not practical. The mirror was placed so that it was in the way of the person looking through the tube. Newton drew a sketch that solved this problem. He placed the mirror at an angle and put a hole for the eyepiece in the side of the tube.

Newton decided to make a telescope to test his idea. His boyhood skill in making models was now being put to good use, but he had a difficult task ahead of him. He had to make everything for himself, even the curved mirrors and lenses. There were no scientific supply catalogs or stores where he could buy what he needed.

The reflecting telescope was a huge success. It was very small, only eight inches long. It gave a clearer and larger image than bigger telescopes of the old type. Newton studied the planets through his telescope. He demonstrated its power to Dr. Barrow.

In 1671, Barrow took the little telescope to London. He showed it to several important people, including King Charles II, who was anxious to keep up with advances in science. The

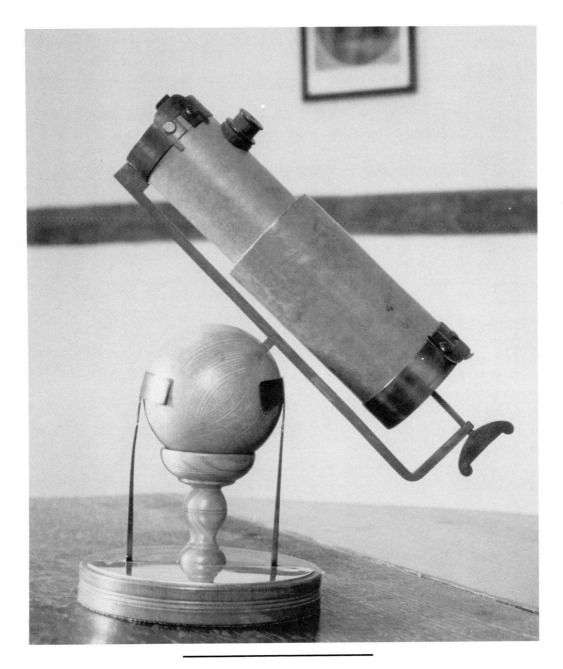

Newton's telescope

reflecting telescope was also shown at a meeting of the Royal Society. Everyone was impressed. Henry Oldenberg, the secretary of the Society, wrote a description of it. He sent the description to the leading scientists of Europe.

Newton was pleased that his invention caused so much excitement. He was even more pleased when he was invited to become a member of the Royal Society in 1672. At the meeting at which Newton was voted in as a member, a letter was read describing an accurate method for measuring the earth. Newton must not have been aware of this. Otherwise he surely would have reworked his calculations on the orbit of the moon.

The excitement over his telescope drew Newton out of his shell. He decided to share his ideas about light and color. He explained his theories to Oldenberg in a letter that was read aloud at the next meeting of the Royal Society. Once again, everyone was impressed. The Society decided to publish the letter as a scientific paper, but first the experiments were to be repeated by three members. Two of the people chosen to repeat the experiments were well-known physicists. One was Robert Hooke; the other was Robert Boyle.

Robert Hooke was seven years older than Isaac Newton. The two men had a lot in common. Both had brilliant minds. Both had had difficult, lonely childhoods. Newton outgrew some of his early setbacks. He was now in good health and of average height. Robert Hooke was not so fortunate. He was troubled by sickness all his life. He was very short and had a crooked spine. We have no portrait of him, but Samuel Pepys painted a picture in words. He wrote that Hooke "is the most and promises the least of any man in the world that I ever saw."[2]

Hooke had the right background to judge Newton's experiments. He was interested in how light travels. He had published a paper on the wave theory. Newton's color theory was not based on how light travels, but he mentioned in his letter that he did not lean toward the wave theory. Hooke jumped on this point. Newton's feelings were hurt. He thought it was unfair of Hooke to focus on a side issue.

The quarrel between the two men became heated. Newton said he would never publish anything again. He even said he did not want to belong to the Royal Society. Henry Oldenberg, the secretary, tried to calm Newton down. He wrote to him, saying that the membership "esteem and love you."[3]

This was not enough to win Newton back. He shut himself away in Cambridge.

The Hermit Professor

ISAAC NEWTON STILL SHARED ROOMS with John Wickins in Trinity College. As a fellow, he now had his own money to spend. His accounts show that he bought a leather carpet for the main room. He built a workbench and bought tools. He and Wickins chose a new couch together.

In spite of living in the middle of a busy university, Newton led a solitary life. He mostly ate in his own room. When he did join the other professors in the college dining room, he was often lost in thought. Sometimes he forgot to eat. If someone asked him a question he usually had

A portrait of the patron of Trinity College, Henry VIII, hangs above the dining hall.

a good answer, but he never started a conversation. Nor did he laugh much. For five years he had a secretary, who only heard him laugh once in all that time. Isaac had lent a friend a copy of Euclid's geometry. The friend asked what good studying Euclid would do. This question made Newton "very merry."[1]

Newton's accounts also show that he spent money on a tablecloth and six napkins, but he did not entertain much. When he did have visitors to his rooms, he was not always a great host. One time he went to his study to get a bottle of wine. A thought came to him, and he forgot all about his company. He sat down at his desk and lost himself in his work.

Newton was very untidy. He rarely changed his clothes. He did not bother to comb his long hair, which was silvery gray by the time he was thirty. Nor did he fasten his shoes. Newton had no hobbies. He did not go out riding, walking, or bowling, or get any other exercise. Any time away from his studies was time lost.

Quite likely, the students and other professors

made fun of the eccentric professor, yet they also respected him. He used to draw diagrams in the gravel of the garden paths. For days afterward, people carefully walked around the sketches.

Although Newton was famous for his brilliant mind, students did not flock to hear his lectures. He was required to give one lecture a week. Very few people attended; sometimes no one was there. Newton's secretary wrote that "few went to hear him, and fewer yet understood him" and that often "for want of hearers, he read to the walls."[2]

After Newton's quarrel with Robert Hooke over his paper on light, he buried himself in his work. He was impatient with any interruption, even letters. He answered one letter saying that he was busy with some "business of my own which at present takes up all my time and thoughts." He ended the letter with the words, "I am in great haste, Yours. . . ."[3]

What was keeping Isaac Newton so busy?

It was not mathematics. He now had a new interest; he was spending all his time on chemistry. He had been reading the works of Robert Boyle.

He bought flasks, glass tubes, and chemicals, and he built two furnaces in the rooms he shared with John Wickins. Wickins seems to have been a very tolerant man. He sometimes even helped Newton with his experiments.

Newton's interest in chemistry led him to a much older subject called alchemy. Alchemy was closely related to chemistry, but it also involved magic and spells. One goal of alchemy was to turn nonprecious metals into gold. However, it was not the search for a way to make gold that interested Newton. He wanted to understand the nature of life itself. He thought that some clue to the nature of life was hidden in the writings of the early alchemists. He spent years making notes from ancient texts, repeating old experiments, and concocting strange medicines.

Newton did not publish any papers on his alchemy experiments. The information we have on his studies is all from his notebooks and loose sheets of paper, which are not easy to read. He kept correcting his notes by writing on top of what he had already written. He sometimes wrote

The mathematical bridge over the River Cam was constructed by Isaac Newton.

upside down between the lines. He would switch from Latin to English and then back to Latin again. It is hard to tell his own thoughts from notes that he took while reading.

Isaac Newton's papers were left to his heirs. When they first offered his alchemy notes to

Cambridge, the university did not want them. It made people uncomfortable that England's greatest scientist had dabbled in magic. Fifty years later, the notes were accepted. To this day, they make many people uneasy, yet the papers do show the range of the questions that Isaac Newton's great mind explored.

Newton also spent a great deal of time studying the Bible. He was very interested in the history of religion. Although he was deeply religious, he did not accept all the beliefs of the Church of England. This almost cost him his career at Cambridge, which was closely tied to the Church of England. Every new professor had to become a minister within seven years. If Newton did not do so, he would have to give up his fellowship. Isaac Barrow went to see the king on his friend's behalf. In 1675, Barrow secured an agreement that Newton could be a professor without taking holy orders.

With another crisis behind him, Isaac Newton again buried himself in his studies of alchemy, religion, and mathematics.

A Question of Gravity

ROBERT HOOKE BECAME THE SECRETARY of the Royal Society in 1678. His job was to plan meetings and to keep in touch with members. He sent Isaac Newton a letter giving him news of the scientific world. He asked what Newton was doing these days.

Newton wrote back, saying he was involved in "other business."[1] Perhaps when he reread the letter, he thought it sounded unfriendly. He added an experiment for Hooke to try. The problem was to find the path of an object falling toward the center of the earth, taking into account that the earth is spinning. Newton included a sketch of the falling object.

When Hooke looked at the sketch, he noticed an error. He lost no time in pointing it out. Newton never did like to be told he was wrong, especially not by Robert Hooke. However, he answered Hooke's letter politely.

This led to more letters from Hooke. Newton ignored them, but they did remind him of his earlier calculations on the orbit of the moon. By this time he knew that he had not been using the correct distance for the radius of the earth. He redid his calculations. Even before he was finished, he could tell that he could explain the moon's orbit around the earth. He became so excited that his hand shook too much to complete the arithmetic. He had to have someone else do it for him.

Even though Newton was excited about his results, he did not rush out and tell everyone. Instead, he shoved the calculations into a drawer.

The following May, sadness touched Isaac Newton's life. His half-brother, Benjamin, came

Hannah Newton Smith was buried in Colsterworth Church in 1679.

down with a fever. Hannah Smith nursed her son
back to health. While doing so, she caught the
fever and became very ill. The family sent for
Isaac, who came home and stayed at his mother's
bedside until her death. He "sate up whole nights

with her, gave her all her Physick himself, and dressed all her blisters with his own hands. . ."[2]

Isaac Newton then had the sad duty of arranging for his mother's funeral. She was buried in the Colsterworth churchyard beside his father. In her will she left small sums of money to her other children, Mary, Hannah, and Benjamin. They had already inherited money from their father. Most of her property, including Woolsthorpe Manor, went to Isaac.

Some of the land was rented out. One of Newton's tenants was Edward Storer, with whom he had lived while he attended school in Grantham. Storer turned out to be a troublesome tenant. He was always behind in the rent, and he ignored Newton's letters. Eight years later, Newton was still having problems with Storer, who had neglected the buildings and fences, and had not paid his rent.

Newton was on good terms with Edward Storer's brother, Arthur, who must have forgiven Newton for rubbing his face against the church wall. He had left England and now lived in

Christopher Wren (1632–1723) was a founding member of the Royal Society.

Maryland. He was interested in astronomy. He and Newton wrote each other letters about the stars.

In 1684, a conversation in a London coffee house had a big effect on Isaac Newton's career. Robert Hooke sat talking with his friends Christopher Wren and Edmund Halley. They were discussing the movement of the planets. They agreed with the German astronomer Johannes

Edmund Halley (1656–1742) said that the orbit of a comet is also an ellipse. He correctly predicted when the comet of 1682 would return, and the comet is now called Halley's comet.

Kepler that planets travel in an ellipse, but could anyone prove this mathematically?

Christopher Wren said he would give a prize to anyone who could prove it within two months. The prize was to be a book worth forty shillings. The proof would be recorded and published. Hooke said he could provide the answer, but he would not tell them yet. He wanted Halley to try, so that he would know how difficult the problem was.

Although Halley gave the problem some thought, he was sure he could not win the prize. Two months passed, and Hooke did not claim the prize either. Halley was disappointed. Having proof that the inverse-square law applied to the planets would help him with his observations in astronomy. He decided that the one person who could solve the problem was Isaac Newton. He told Wren that he planned to visit the hermit scientist.

Without wasting any more time, Halley set off for Cambridge. He went straight to Newton's rooms and asked what the path of a planet would be if the inverse-square law were true. Newton answered that it would be an ellipse. When Halley then asked him how he could be so sure, Newton calmly said he had already proved it.

He could not find the important calculation, however. It was now several years since he had shoved it into a drawer. He promised to rework the problem and send it to Halley in London.

In November 1684, Halley received the proof he had been waiting for. It came in the form of a nine-page paper written in Latin. In his hands, Halley held the answer to the question of why planets travel around the sun in an ellipse. He was overawed by Isaac Newton. Newton had made a tremendously important discovery, but he had not bothered to tell anyone about it.

We owe Edmund Halley a great debt. If he had not made that trip to Cambridge, it is hard to say how long Newton's results would have stayed hidden.

8

The *Principia*

ISAAC NEWTON'S SHORT PAPER ON THE movement of the planets seemed to trigger the creative forces in his great brain. His mind again became totally focused on mathematics, and he decided to expand the paper into a book. Soon Newton's life was taken over by his writing. Meals were not important; he mostly snacked on bread and water. He never sat down at the dining table. Nor did he go to bed at night; he took short naps without undressing. He became sloppier than ever. However, that did not matter much, because he rarely left his rooms. The only thing that he cared about was getting his thoughts onto paper. He was exact and logical in doing that.

Newton returned to the questions that had interested him as he sat under the apple tree in the garden at Woolsthorpe. Gravity pulled on an apple falling toward the earth. It pulled on the planets as they journeyed around the sun. It pulled on a bullet fired from a gun.

Newton's mind took another giant leap forward. Not only did the earth pull on the apple; the apple also pulled on the earth. The amount of pull depended on its mass. (Mass is the amount of matter in an object.) This led to Newton's universal law of gravitation: Every particle in the universe is attracted to every other particle. The force of their attraction is related to their masses and their distance apart from each other. All the motion in the solar system obeys the same law.

Newton needed data to prove his law. He wrote to John Flamsteed, the Royal Astronomer. Flamsteed sent him figures on the position of stars and on the orbits of the planets.

Mathematical Principles of Natural Philosophy is

the English title of Newton's book. (Natural philosophy is now called physics.) It is mostly known as the *Principia*. He wrote it in Latin, and there are three volumes. Newton finished the first volume before Easter of 1685, and the second volume was completed by late summer. He spent several months revising them and then sent them to Halley at the Royal Society.

The Society had just published a *History of Fishes*. This was a big, expensive volume. There was no money left to pay for Newton's book. Halley, not a wealthy man, offered to put up his own money to publish it. His father had just died without leaving a will. Until the estate was settled, his income came from the Royal Society. Because the Society was so short of money, he had just been paid with fifty copies of *Fishes*. However, he made the arrangements to publish Newton's book, acted as editor, and carefully checked all the diagrams.

At this point, Newton and Robert Hooke got into another quarrel. Hooke claimed he had thought of the inverse-square law first. Even if he

PHILOSOPHIÆ

NATURALIS

PRINCIPIA

MATHEMATICA.

Autore *JS. NEWTON,* *Trin. Coll. Cantab. Soc.* Matheseos
Professore *Lucasiano,* & Societatis Regalis Sodali.

IMPRIMATUR·
S. PEPYS, *Reg. Soc.* PRÆSES.
Julii 5. 1686.

LONDINI,

Jussu *Societatis Regiæ* ac Typis *Josephi Streater.* Prostat apud
plures Bibliopolas. *Anno* MDCLXXXVII.

The title page of the Principia.

had, he had not done the mathematics to prove the law. No one except Newton took Hooke's claim seriously. Newton became very upset, and said he would not finish volume three.

Halley was stunned. Without volume three, the first two volumes probably would not sell. Halley would end up seriously in debt, but that was not his main concern. He did not want Isaac Newton's great work to be incomplete. Halley wrote a tactful letter, and Newton agreed to go back to work.

The *Principia* was published on July 5, 1687, as a Royal Society publication. Samuel Pepys was president of the Society at this time, and his name was on the cover above the date. The nine-page letter that Newton had written in answer to Halley's question had grown to 511 pages. Bound in leather, it sold for nine shillings.

The book was not easy to read, but it sold well. People recognized that it was a very important work, although they did not know how lasting its importance would be. The *Principia* contains Newton's three laws of motion. These laws are the

Law I

Law II

Law III

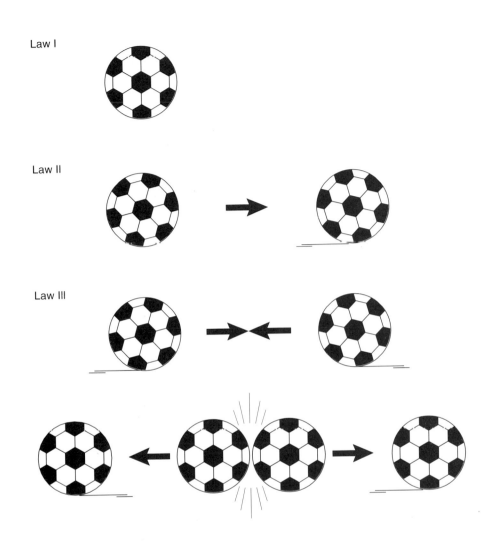

Using soccer balls can help explain Newton's laws of motion. Law I shows that if no force acts on the soccer ball, it will not move. Law II shows that the soccer ball will move when a force acts upon it. In the case of Law III, if two balls are pushed towards each other, they will bounce off one another and travel in the opposite direction. That is, there will be an opposite reaction.

foundation of the science of mechanics. They apply both to simple machines and to rockets that blast spaceships into orbit.

Newton's three laws of motion state:

1. Every object stays at rest unless it is acted on by an outside force. If it is in motion, it travels in a straight line unless it is acted on by an outside force.

2. The outside force is related to the direction and the increase in speed of the object.

3. To every action there is an opposite and equal reaction.

In volume 3 of the *Principia,* Newton showed how his theory applied to moons, planets, and comets. He explained the earth's tides. He said that because the earth spins, it is not completely round; it is flattened at the poles. An expedition to Lapland proved this to be true nine years after Newton's death.

Halley was excited about Newton's observations on comets. If, as he said, the orbit of a comet was an ellipse, then the comet should be seen from the earth at regular intervals. A very bright comet had appeared in 1682. Halley began to search old

Halley's Comet

records to find when bright comets had been seen in the past. He worked on the problem for over twenty years. He knew that Johannes Kepler had described a bright comet in 1607. In old manuscripts, he found that comets had appeared in 1531 and in 1456. He decided that the same comet was showing up at seventy-six-year intervals. He predicted that the 1682 comet would return in 1758. He did not live to see it, but when it was seen in 1758, the comet was named after him. In this century, Halley's Comet appeared in 1910 and 1986.

Charles II died two years before the *Principia* was published. He might not have understood it, but he would have been interested. A copy was presented to his brother James II, who was now king, but James did not care about science.

James was not the only person unexcited about the *Principia*. While Newton was walking through Trinity College, one of his students pointed to him and said, "There goes the man that writt a book that neither he nor anybody else understands."[1]

Outside Forces

UNTIL HE WAS FORTY-FIVE, ISAAC Newton's life followed a straight line. The "sober, silent, thinking lad" became a sober, silent, thinking man. Then, with the *Principia* almost finished, his life took off in a new direction. The outside force that caused this change in direction was the king of England himself.

King James II wrote to John Peachell at Cambridge, asking him to award a master of arts degree to Father Albin Francis, a monk. Francis would not have to "performe the Exercises" or take "any Oath or Oaths whatsoever."[1]

Some of the university officials wanted to fulfill the king's request. They thought they should bend the rules this one time. For the first time, Isaac Newton became involved in university politics. He said that they must stand firm. If King James were allowed to get involved in university affairs, there was no saying where it would end. Newton convinced the officials not to do the king's bidding.

When James heard that the university would not do as he asked, he ordered John Peachell to appear in court. Judge Jeffreys, who was to hear the case, was known as a "hanging judge." He was both brutal and unfair.

The university chose eight professors to accompany Peachell, and Newton was one of them. Jeffreys could tell that Peachell was timid and ill prepared. He aimed all his remarks at Peachell, who became so nervous that he could not put up a good defense. The judge found Peachell guilty of disobedience and stripped him of his job. The other professors, who never got the chance to speak, got off lightly. Jeffreys dismissed them with a threat. He told them, "Go your way, and sin no more, lest a worse thing come unto you."[2]

Albin Francis did not get his master's degree, however. James II did nothing about it. By this time, he had troubles of his own. In the summer of 1688, his second wife gave birth to a son. James already had a grown-up daughter, Mary. She was a Protestant and was married to Prince William in Holland. Until the baby boy was born, she had been next in line to the throne. Some English people were not happy that there was now a new heir who would be brought up as a Catholic.

In November, William came over from Holland with six hundred ships to invade England. James II fled to France. Most people were glad to see him go. They called William's takeover the Glorious Revolution because no blood was shed. People had been afraid of another civil war.

After Newton's success in university affairs, he got into national politics. He ran for Parliament, and he was elected to represent the university in 1689.

Newton was a member of Parliament for just one year, but it turned out to be an important

William of Orange and his wife Mary, daughter of James II, were invited by Parliament to take over the throne of England in 1688. Since then, every ruler of England has been a Protestant.

year. He took part in the vote that proclaimed William and Mary to be king and queen of England. He voted on the Bill of Rights, which limited the power of the king and gave more rights to citizens. It became the model for the first ten amendments of the Constitution of the United States. The Toleration Act, which was passed while Newton was a member, granted English people more religious freedom than they had before. Although Newton voted for these new laws, he did not take part in the debates. In fact, there is only one record of him saying anything all year—when he asked an usher to close the window!

In the fall of 1693, Isaac Newton had severe health problems. He suffered a mental breakdown. He sent strange letters to friends, accusing them of plotting against him.

In a letter to Samuel Pepys, he wrote, "I must withdraw from your acquaintance, and see neither you nor the rest of my friends any more."[3] Pepys was worried when he read the letter. He asked a friend in Cambridge to check up on Newton. Isaac told this friend that he remembered sending the letter although he now had no idea what was in it. He had written it after not sleeping for five nights in a row.

News of Isaac Newton's breakdown spread all through Europe. Some said it was caused by his losing some of his papers in a fire. (This often happened when people wrote by candlelight.) Others said that Newton was paying the price for years of overwork.

A recent theory is that he may have been

The modern Houses of Parliament in London were completed in 1867. When Isaac Newton was a member of Parliament, meetings were held in St. Stephen's Chapel in Westminster Palace. The palace was destroyed by fire in 1834, but the chapel survived and can still be seen today.

suffering from mercury poisoning. He used mercury, then called quicksilver, in his chemistry and alchemy experiments. Some of the symptoms of mercury poisoning are loss of memory and not being able to sleep or eat. Bleeding gums and loose teeth are also symptoms. Newton did not have that symptom, however; he had healthy teeth.

Newton himself joked about the effect of mercury. His hair was silvery gray by the time he was thirty. When John Wickins claimed that his friend's hair was gray because he worked so hard, Newton said it was because of "the Experiments he made so often with Quick Silver."[4]

We probably never will know what caused Newton's Black Year. Mental illness is often hard to explain. It is almost impossible to explain an illness that took place three hundred years ago.

By 1696, Newton was completely well. He was ready to take on new challenges. His life took off in yet another direction. This time the outside force was the offer of a job; Isaac Newton was asked to be Warden of the Mint.

The Mint

ON BECOMING WARDEN OF THE MINT IN 1696, Isaac Newton moved to London, which would be his home for the next thirty years. During his long life, Newton did very little traveling. Lincolnshire, Cambridge, and London were the only places he knew, but that did not limit his journeys of the mind.

The letter that offered Newton the job as warden stated that "[it] has not too much bus'ness to require more attendance than you may spare. . ."[1] In other words, he would not need to work very hard. The person who was head of the Mint was the master, not the warden. The warden did not have to make decisions. Newton, however, was not someone who did things by halves. He always took work seriously.

When Newton became the warden, the coin system in England was in a state of crisis. Before Charles II became king in 1660, coins were made by hand. Handmade coins were not completely round, and the faces on the coins often were off center. Because coins were not uniform, it was easy for people to counterfeit them. Counterfeit (fake) coins were almost as plentiful as real ones. Another common way of cheating was to clip or shave the edges of silver coins. With its edges clipped, a coin still looked much the same and could be used. The clippings and shavings were melted down and sold as pure silver.

Making coins by machine was supposed to solve these problems. Machine-made coins had marked or milled edges. This would put the clippers out of business. It would be easy to see if a coin had been clipped. The new coins presented a new problem, though. The silver they were made from was worth more than the value of the coin. People melted them down, and new coins disappeared almost as soon as they were minted. Meanwhile, people still squabbled over the old clipped and counterfeit coins. Everyone was eager to spend them, but no one wanted to accept them.

Shortly before Newton became the warden, Parliament voted to call in all the old money. The Mint would make enough new coins to replace it. People at the Mint had to work overtime to make enough new coins to replace the old ones. The early shift started at 4:00 A.M., and the last shift ended at midnight. This was a big job. It was also expensive; a tax was levied to pay for the recoinage. The tax was based on the number of windows in each house. Owners of big houses with lots of windows paid higher taxes. To reduce their taxes, some people sealed up windows. This happened at Woolsthorpe. One of the windows in the room where Newton was born was blocked off. Little Isaac's carvings on the windowsill were covered over. They came to light years later when the window was unblocked.

The Mint was located in the Tower of London when Isaac Newton was warden.

The Mint was located between the outer and the inner walls of the Tower of London. The buildings included workshops, stores, stables, and the warden's house. The warden's house faced a high wall. It was gloomy and noisy.

The house also had a terrible odor. A lot of the machinery at the Mint was turned by horses. The annual bill for disposing of horse manure was seven hundred pounds.

After a few weeks, Newton decided to move. He bought a house on Jermyn Street and set about furnishing it. He chose red drapes, a red couch, and red hangings. He invited his niece, Catherine Barton, to be his hostess and housekeeper. Catherine was the daughter of his half-sister Hannah. She was a witty and beautiful young woman.

Isaac Newton became very fond of Catherine. A letter written to her when she was ill shows his concern. A year or two after she moved to London, Catherine caught smallpox. She was away visiting friends in the country at the time. Newton wrote, "Pray let me know by the next how your face is, and if the fever be going. Perhaps warm milk from the cow may help to abate it. I am your very loving uncle, Is. Newton."[2] Catherine recovered completely.

Newton entertained more in London than he did in Cambridge, but he still liked to live quietly. He did not go out much to concerts or to the theater; he spent most of his spare time reading and studying. After attending the opera, he said, "The first act gave me the greatest pleasure. The second quite tired me: at the third I ran away."[3]

Meantime, things were going well at the Mint. Isaac Newton had the right skills for the job. He was good at problem solving, and he had no trouble mastering the accounting system. From his studies in alchemy, he knew about the nature of metal, and he knew how to combine metals to make alloys.

In 1700, Isaac became Master of the Mint. He was now head of the whole operation. Never before had a warden been promoted to master.

"The Great Ocean of Truth"

WHEN ISAAC NEWTON FIRST MOVED TO London, he was very busy at the Mint. He did not attend meetings of the Royal Society. The programs at the meetings at that time were quite dull. Besides, Robert Hooke would have been there. Newton still did not get along with him. After Hooke's death, Newton became active in the Society. He was elected president in 1703, and his fame attracted new members and revived an interest in science.

With the Mint running smoothly, Newton now had time for his own work. In 1704, he published a book, *Opticks,* that contained his early experiments on light and color. He also revised the *Principia*. For his new edition, Newton needed more records on the position of the moon. John Flamsteed, who had helped him earlier, sent him the information. When Flamsteed found some mistakes in the figures he had sent, he sent new figures. Newton grew annoyed when the figures kept changing. Flamsteed was not happy either; he wanted to know what Newton was doing with the data. He resented Newton's impatience and the way he demanded more and more information. This led to a quarrel between the two men that went on for years.

Meantime, Newton was still arguing with Wilhelm Leibniz over who deserved the credit for inventing calculus. One of Leibniz's friends sent Newton a mathematical problem. Scientists often exchanged puzzles and problems. However, the friend may have been hoping to stump Newton so he could say that Newton was not as sharp as he used to be.

The problem was waiting for Newton when he came home at four o'clock in the afternoon.

John Flamsteed's telescope is on display at the Royal Observatory.

He was tired after a hard day at the Mint. Nevertheless, he went straight to work on the problem. He worked through the night and had it solved by four in the morning. He sent his calculations back without signing his name, but Leibniz's friend knew who had come up with the answer. He said, "The lion is recognized by its print."[1]

In 1705, Isaac was greatly honored when Queen Anne made him a knight. The event took place at Trinity College in Cambridge. The farm lad from Lincolnshire had come a long way; he was now Sir Isaac Newton.

Newton's biographer William Stukeley, also from Lincolnshire, was a student at Cambridge at this time. He went on to become a doctor in London. He joined the Royal Society, where he met his hero, Isaac Newton, who invited Stukeley to his home. The two men became friends. Newton enjoyed talking about his old school days in Grantham. Without Stukeley's biography, we would not know much about Newton's childhood.

John Conduitt was another young man who

was close to Newton in his old age. Conduitt, who married Newton's niece Catherine in 1717, collected stories about his famous uncle-in-law. He kept notes on all their conversations.

Newton enjoyed good health until almost the end of his long life. He looked young for a man in his eighties. His white hair remained thick. He had strong teeth and keen eyesight. A few days before his death, the rector (priest) visited him. Afterward the rector wrote that he found Newton writing "without the help of spectacles, at the greatest distance of the room from the windows, and with a parcel of books on the table, casting a shade upon the paper. Seeing this, I said to him, 'Sir, you seem to be writing in a place where you cannot so well see.' His answer was, 'A little light serves me.'"[2]

In January 1725, Isaac Newton came down with a bad cough. Catherine thought it was caused by the smoky air in London. She persuaded him to move out to Kensington. The air was fresher in the country. Today, Kensington is in the middle of London.

Isaac Newton's statue stands in Trinity College, Cambridge.

Newton still went to meetings of the Royal Society, though not regularly. The last meeting he attended was on March 2, 1727. By the time he got back to Kensington two days later, he was very ill. He died on March 20 at the age of eighty-four.

The minutes of the Royal Society for March 23 read, "The Chair being Vacant by the Death of Sir Isaac Newton there was no Meeting this Day."[3]

Isaac Newton was honored in death, as he had been in life. He was buried in Westminster Abbey, where a huge monument was erected in his memory. The text on the monument reads, "Let Mortals rejoice that there has existed so great an Ornament to the Human Race."

Isaac Newton summed up his own life more simply. Shortly before he died, he told a friend, "I don't know what I may seem to the world, but, as to myself, I seem to have been only like a boy playing on the sea shore, and diverting myself in now and then finding a smoother pebble or a prettier shell than ordinary, [while] the great ocean of truth lay all undiscovered before me."[4]

Experiments— Light and Weighty

THE KEY TO ISAAC NEWTON'S GENIUS WAS his power of thought. He once explained that when he was faced with a problem he kept it in his mind until he solved it. He often went without food or sleep until he was satisfied with his answer. Few people in the history of the world have been gifted with such powers of concentration.

In this chapter, you will find a few experiments to challenge your mind. In some, you are left to find the answer for yourself. Your parents may not let you skip meals and stay up late until you are satisfied with your answers. They may not think that you are a genius at work—but Isaac Newton's mother did not appreciate that her child was a genius, either!

Newton's Rings—The Color of Light

Sometimes you can see the colors of the rainbow in an oily puddle. These rings of color are known as Newton's Rings. You can also see them in a soap bubble.

Newton used a prism he bought at Sturbridge Fair to break up light into separate colors. You can do this same experiment with a baking pan and a small mirror.

Materials

- a baking pan
- a small rectangular mirror
- a white sheet of paper
- an index card with a pinhole in it

Procedure

1. Fill the pan with water.

2. Lean a mirror against the edge of the pan with its lower half in the water.

3. Place the pan so that the sun shines on the mirror.

4. On a white sheet of paper, catch the rainbow of light that is reflected from the mirror.

5. You can isolate the colors, just as Newton did, by holding the index card an inch or two in front of the white paper and moving it up and down so that a pinpoint of red, yellow, or blue light passes through the hole and shines on the paper.

To see the colors on soap bubbles, add a little sugar to a detergent or soap bubble solution. This lets you blow bigger bubbles. How does the size of the bubble affect the brightness of the color?

Where else can you see rainbows? What makes a double rainbow?

Making a Paddle Wheel

Instead of minding the sheep, Newton made waterwheels. A machine that turns by water power requires a paddle wheel. Try making your own paddle wheel.

Materials

- an empty spool of thread
- six one-inch squares of index card or light cardboard
- glue
- a pencil or stick thin enough to pass through the hole in the spool. The spool should turn freely.

Procedure

1. Bend a quarter of an inch inward along one edge of each square.

2. Glue the bent edge of the first square to the spool and let it dry.

3. Repeat this with the other squares, placing them at equal distances around the spool.

4. Insert the pencil or stick through the spool as an axle.

5. Now hold your waterwheel under a dripping faucet.

What happens when you increase the flow of water? Does the distance of the paddle wheel from the faucet affect the speed at which the wheel turns?

Using Your Marbles

Challenge your friends to move a marble from one paper cup to another without touching either the marble or the cups. Then show them that it can be done with the help of the force of gravity.

Materials

- a marble
- two five-ounce paper cups
- masking tape
- a yard stick

Procedure

1. Cut one cup down so that the sides are about one inch tall.

2. Tape this cup to one end of the yardstick and place the marble in it.

3. Tape the taller cup about four inches along the yardstick from the first.

4. Tape the other end of the yardstick to the door frame at floor level. The tape forms a hinge so that the stick can be raised.

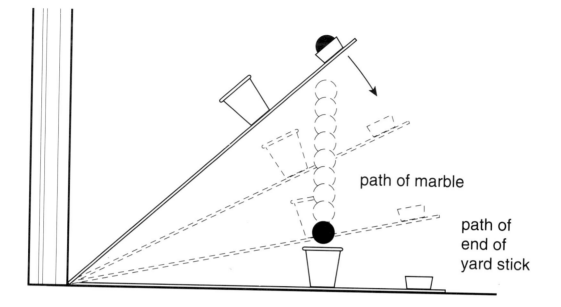

path of marble

path of
end of
yard stick

5. Raise the end of the yardstick until it is about twenty inches above the floor.

6. You are now ready to move the marble without touching either cup.

7. Release the yardstick with a light downward push.

The marble should fall into the other cup. How does this come about? The marble falls in a straight line under the force of gravity. The cups follow a curved path, as is shown in the diagram.

It may take a little practice to push down with the exact force so that the marble lands in the other cup. If the marble falls short of the cup, give a stronger push. If it goes too far, push down less hard.

Defying Gravity

Here is a demonstration that seems to go against the law of gravity.

Materials

- two cones or funnels
- masking tape
- two sticks or dowels
- two books of different sizes

Procedure:

1. Join the flat surfaces of the cones or funnels with tape.

2. Stand the books on their sides.

3. Place the sticks across the two books, so that they are farther apart on the taller book (see diagram).

4. Place the double cone at the bottom of the slope.

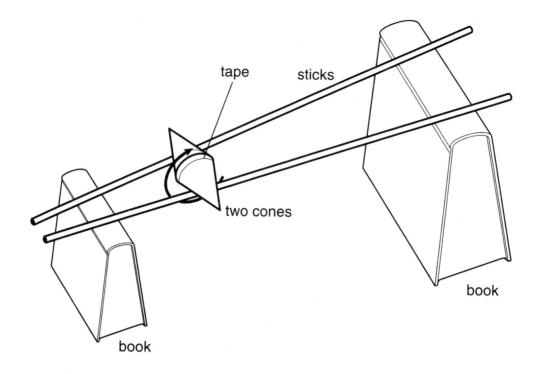

tape

sticks

two cones

book

book

The cones roll uphill! What's going on?

Although the cones seem to be moving upward, their center of gravity is actually moving downwards. A body's center of gravity is the point around which its weight is balanced. The cones are really sinking lower between the sticks.

The Age of Miracles

We live in an age of miracles beyond anything Isaac Newton dreamed of. Take a look around you at all the things that would baffle the great mind of science. When Newton studied optics, he never guessed that surgeons would someday use laser beams of light to do operations. Newton spent years thinking about magic and alchemy. The alchemist's goal was to change other metals into gold. Nuclear scientists can now do this, though it is too costly to be worth it.

Isaac Newton's genius was not just based on answering questions. It was based on asking them. He wondered why an apple falls toward the earth. He wondered what keeps the moon up in the sky. He questioned things that everyone else took for granted. If he were alive today, he would approach science in the same way as he did three hundred years ago. He would not take any of the miracles that surround us for granted.

Questions come before answers in great discoveries.

Chronology

1642—Isaac Newton, the elder, dies in October. Isaac Newton is born at Woolsthorpe Manor on December 25.

1642–1646—English Civil War.

1646—Hannah Newton marries Barnabas Smith.

1649—Charles I is beheaded and Oliver Cromwell becomes Lord Protector of England.

1655—Isaac starts grammar school in Grantham.

1660—The Restoration: The monarchy is restored and Charles II becomes king.

1661—Isaac enters Trinity College, Cambridge.

1665—The plague breaks out in London.

1665–1666—Isaac Newton's "miracle years."

1666—The Great Fire of London.

1667—Newton is made a fellow at Trinity College.

1669—Newton is appointed professor of mathematics.

1672—Newton is made a member of the Royal Society.

1679—Hannah Newton Smith dies.

1684—Newton returns to the study of gravity.

1687—Publication of the *Principia.*

1688—The Glorious Revolution. James II flees England and William III and Mary II become joint rulers.

1689—Newton becomes a member of Parliament.

1693—Newton suffers a mental breakdown.

1696—Newton moves to London as Warden of the Mint.

1700—Newton is appointed Master of the Mint.

1703—Newton becomes president of the Royal Society.

1704—Publication of *Opticks.*

1705—Newton is knighted by Queen Anne.

1727—Newton dies on March 20.

Chapter Notes

Chapter 1

1. John Fauvel, Raymond Flood, Michael Shortland, and Robin Wilson, eds., *Let Newton Be!* (Oxford, England: Oxford University Press, 1988), p. 38.

2. Gale E. Christianson, *In the Presence of the Creator* (New York: Macmillan, 1984), p. 4.

Chapter 2

1. William Stukeley, *Memoirs of Sir Isaac Newton's Life* (London: Taylor and Francis, 1936), p. 46.

2. Ibid.

3. Ibid.

4. Ibid., p. 42.

5. Richard S. Westfall, *Never at Rest* (Cambridge, England: Cambridge University Press, 1980), p. 60.

6. Stukeley, p. 41.

7. Ibid., p. 39.

8. Ibid., p. 51.

Chapter 3

1. Richard S. Westfall, *Never at Rest* (Cambridge, England: Cambridge University Press, 1980), p. 74.

John Wickins's son wrote this in a letter to a friend many years later.

2. Ibid, p. 104.

3. William Stukeley, *Memoirs of Sir Isaac Newton's Life* (London: Taylor and Francis, 1936), p. 53.

Chapter 4

1. Richard S. Westfall, *Never at Rest* (Cambridge, England: Cambridge University Press, 1980), p. 143.

2. William Stukeley, *Memoirs of Sir Isaac Newton's Life* (London: Taylor and Francis, 1936), p. 20.

Chapter 5

1. Gale E. Christianson, *In the Presence of the Creator* (New York: Macmillan, 1984), p. 92.

2. Ibid., p. 157.

3. Ibid., p. 180.

Chapter 6

1. William Stukeley, *Memoirs of Sir Isaac Newton's Life* (London: Taylor and Francis, 1936), p. 57.

2. Richard S. Westfall, *Never at Rest* (Cambridge, England: Cambridge University Press, 1980), p. 209.

3. Ibid., p. 281.

Chapter 7

1. Richard S. Westfall, *Never at Rest* (Cambridge, England: Cambridge University Press, 1980), p. 383.

2. Gale E. Christianson, *In the Presence of the Creator* (New York: Macmillan, 1984), p. 237.

Chapter 8

1. Gale E. Christianson, *In the Presence of the Creator* (New York: Macmillan, 1984), p. 291.

Chapter 9

1. Gale E. Christianson, *In the Presence of the Creator* (New York: Macmillan, 1984), p. 321.

2. Ibid., p. 325.

3. Ibid., p. 356.

4. Richard S. Westfall, *Never at Rest* (Cambridge, England: Cambridge University Press, 1980), p. 196.

Chapter 10

1. H. D. Anthony, *Sir Isaac Newton* (London, New York, Toronto: Abelard-Schuman, 1960), p. 139.

2. Ibid., p. 146.

3. William Stukeley, *Memoirs of Sir Isaac Newton's Life* (London: Taylor and Francis, 1936), p. 14.

Chapter 11

1. Richard S. Westfall, *Never at Rest* (Cambridge, England: Cambridge University Press, 1980), p. 583.

2. Ibid., p. 869.

3. Ibid., p. 870.

4. Ibid., p. 863.

Glossary

alchemy—The forerunner of modern chemistry. Alchemy blended science and magic.

binomial—A mathematical equation with two elements, such as $2x + 3y$.

calculus—The branch of mathematics invented by Isaac Newton. It is used to determine, for example, the area under a curve.

ellipse—A flattened circle, or oval.

fellowship—A position to which a graduate of a university may be elected.

fluxions—The name used by Isaac Newton for calculus, the branch of mathematics he invented.

geometry—The branch of mathematics dealing with lines, flat shapes (e.g., circles, and squares) and solid shapes (e.g., spheres and cubes).

gravity—The attraction or pulling force between one object and another.

inverse square law—As two objects get farther apart the force of attraction between them weakens by one divided by the square of the distance between the objects. This can be written as $1/d^2$, where d is distance.

law—A scientific principle that is universally accepted as fact.

mass—The amount of matter in an object. Mass is different from weight which depends on gravity. You would weigh less on the moon but your mass would still be the same as on earth.

optics—The study of light.

plague—A epidemic of disease, where the rate of death is very high.

prism—A multisided piece of glass or crystal.

reflecting telescope—A telescope that uses two mirrors to give a clearer vision.

sizar—A student at Cambridge University, who worked at the university in order to pay for his room and board.

spectrum—The colors that make up white light. To humans, the visible spectrum is red, orange, yellow, green, blue, indigo, and violet.

theory—A general term for a scientific principle that has been proved by experimentation.

Further Reading

Ardley, Neil. *Light.* New York: Macmillan Books for Young Readers, 1992.

Challoneer, Jack. *The Visual Dictionary of Physics.* New York: Dorling Kindersley, 1995.

Gardener, Robert. *Experiments with Light and Mirrors.* Springfield, N.J.: Enslow Publishers, Inc., 1995.

Nardo, Don. *Gravity: The Universal Force.* San Diego: Lucent Books, 1990.

Spangenburg, Ray and Diane K. Moser. *The History of Science from the Ancient Greeks to the Scientific Revolution.* New York: Facts on File, 1993.

———. *The History of Science in the Eighteenth Century.* New York: Facts on File, 1993.

Stwertka, Albert and Eve Stwertka. *Physics from Newton to the Big Bang.* New York: Franklin Watts, 1986.

Swisher, Clarice. *The Glorious Revolution.* San Diego: Lucent Books, 1996.

Index